When The Mind Speaks

Kushagra Singh

pencil

ISBN 978-93-5610-174-6

Published in India 2022 by Pencil

A brand of
One Point Six Technologies Pvt. Ltd.
123, Building J2, Shram Seva Premises,
Wadala Truck Terminal, Wadala (E)
Mumbai 400037, Maharashtra, INDIA
E connect@thepencilapp.com
W www.thepencilapp.com

Author biography

I am Kushagra, born in the alluring city Banda, UP in India. I love to explore, especially people and myself. I have a keen interest in Psychology and related fields. I am also studying computers.

When writing this book, I am a student who is studying about computers in INFORMATION TECHNOLOGY branch of engineering. I have chosen to study computers and their applications because I am quite interested in their working and logical approach to each and everything. In this field, everything has a genuine reason for happening and I love to explore them.

I also have an interest in psychology and studying the behaviour of people in different life circumstances.

I have also done various courses on psychology and English communication skills, which helped me a lot to create a base in new domains of life.

Courses like ' Introduction to Psychology by Yale University ' and ' Social Psychology by Wesleyan University ' are really helpful.

I hope you will enjoy one of my explorations of mind through this book.

You can find me on in kushagraprofile (https://www.linkedin.com/in/kushagraprofile)

THANK YOU!

CONTENTS

Preface

I am being a student inspired to write a short book as a huge start to widen my learning experience.

I think you should go through this book at least once then I expect you might fall in love with the text and go again and again!

My target audience is anybody. No matter what is age, gender, etc, anybody can read this book. But I expect people who are more engaged and wanted to know more about life should read the book. This might add some value to you.

In this book, you will explore the human mind and a glimpse of Psychology.
As we know, nowadays, how life is actually becoming harder to survive peacefully.

This book will help you explore more about yourself with text and poems.
I have made the content as interactive as possible, you may feel it when you read the book.
The text deals with tour daily life, how to deal with emotions, and to live positive life even if life is going against our flow of living!
I want to share some meaningful knowledge and entertain you. I really hope you would enjoy the content.

Acknowledgements

I am very thankful to my parents and elders for their good wishes and great support during my learning ages.

I am also very thankful to my teachers who played a vital role in making me capable of writing this book.

I am also very thankful to you to consider this book! I really hope it would be a great journey for you with me along with my text.

THANK YOU!

(Kushagra Singh)

A Short to know you...

A beautiful mindset is not born, it is made.

So, you are here to **explore yourself!**

The journey begins here, from this page.

I sometimes wonder how painful it could be for a child, who is never taught to walk! Just imagine, a person who walks on their knees, just for a reason, the person is ignored too much in his or her life results in such a painful beginning of adult life.

As we know, it is our human habit to ignore the importance of time, just from a psychological point of view, like during our childhood, we ignored learning ABC..alphabets, so we were taught forcefully in hundred of ways possible so as a result, when we grow up we can share our thoughts and messages to others and vice versa.

Similarly, the person who walks on his or her knees is now becoming aware of the world!

As we know, the beginning of adulthood is as good as distressing. It is good for people who are loved and cared for but is really a great mess for them, who do not value themself.

Returning back to the person, who was ignored so much, ignoring the cause, let deep dive into the results.

- Since the person is ignored so much, it is for sure, from the quote " ***Every action has the equal and opposite reaction.***", that person must have begged for lots and lots of **attention**and **love**from others.

- Assuming he or she was taught to speak, just take it as a blessing from nature, but is ignored and sometimes bullied by negative people.

The term "Negative People" , I mean the people in one's life, who have only one ambition is to control and downgrade the target person for foolish reasons.

The person is now reaching adulthood, so he is now aware of the importance of walking, But as we know " ***We can not teach an old dog new tricks!***"

I have questions for you!

- What do you think, whether it was a mistake?

Consider the flow of your life, please try to build your thoughts to understand the uncertainity of the question.

- If it was a mistake, then who is responsible for it? OR If it wasn't a mistake, then, Can you explain a reason the person was not able to walk?

If you were that, to whom would you blame. To yourself or society or time or nothing! Because you were just a child, who was not aware of anything. OR If it was just a game of minds!

WE WILL RETURN BACK TO THIS PERSON IN AN UPCOMING CHAPTER

The Mindshift

I love life because

"Nothing is permanent"

so me too.

I am not same,

from one second to other minutes,

That's why I believe in ***permanent***

to be temporary.

The person who is **ignored**and is not able to **walk.** The decent and dangerous example wants to describe our mind. As we grow up, we become mature.

As we become mature, we ignore little **pains**in life.

At a very early age, the person might be normal being unknown to walk. As he was also a kid, fearless and being unaware of upcoming life, but surrounded by **negative people**. Let's assume he or she had **lost their parent**s. I wanted to put the worst example here, sorry for the same.

Just replace the person with your **mind**, negative people with **awful thoughts**, and parents with some **positive and nurturing thoughts**.

From a psychology point of view, **"It is in human genes to give priority to negative thoughts."**

What should be done to prevent this from our life? No matter how fulfilled one is, the person always sees temptation as a priority and ignores all that must be valued first.

So, what is the definition of being positive? The above statement stops us to see new things in life. Without temptation, how we would grow.

We need to even use this to our benefit.

What actually needs to be controlled are the tempting thoughts that result in harming oneself or others.

There are moments in our life when we enjoy ignoring all tensions of life. And other, thinking about what we had lost and what to get to fulfil our happiness.

So, it is necessary to train our mind as it is also growing with us and also has life equivalent to us.

Strategy of thoughts

Nowadays, **humanity** is becoming an **ideal case.**

From Newton's law of gravity, I have drawn the following statement:

No prayers can stop a falling pen due to **gravity.** Untill, some action is taken.

This is the fact that once something is falling, one cannot control it through thoughts. We are not blessed with wizard powers.

So, we take action to catch it before it falls completely.

Similarly, it applies to our thoughts. Yes, **prayers add positivity to life**, but I ruined it to give the most simple example possible. So, in the case of feelings and thoughts, **meditation plays a very vital role**.

But, we will dive some deeper to understand the functioning, To keep it simple, the following theory is inspired by **MEMORY ALLOCATION IN COMPUTERS!**

1. ***Static Feelings***

These are straight forward and a person having this type of feeling makes decisions faster but most of them are independent of the past. This type of person is free from past trauma of life. So, how to be static.

Let's see how the computer is static in the case of memory. In static memory allocation, once the value gets updated then the previous value is lost, even if reinitialized in a certain loop.

So, to attain the quality of being static, don't take tension of previous trauma or negatives in life.

Today, nobody is taking tension, why did you fall down when you were learning to walk!

These feelings work on the principle of temporal locality. What is recent actually affects the most. People having this type of feeling are emotionally stable in most cases.

2. ***Dynamic Feelings***

These feelings are dynamic that is fully dependent on emotions and are controlled by. Anybody, who acquires this type of feeling is driven through various new emotions that are even not present in static.

These types of people live in the way, creating linkage from one life stage to other. They remember the past throughout their life, which is more meaningful than static people.

But sometimes, if there is trauma in their life, makes them pass through negative phases.

But they are actually efficient to manage them as they observe it as a life lesson more than a negative that pulls them to do negative things with themselves.

ADVANTAGES & DISADVANTAGES

Static Feelings

The disadvantage of having static feelings is a person is most of the time **very direct**. The actions are performed without much thinking about the impact.

The advantage is stability in emotions is achieved faster. It may vary from person to person.

Dynamic Feelings

The disadvantage of having dynamic feelings is **decision-making time**. Since, emotion matters, its impact on the future and the maximum of the past events that may have occurred are considered very seriously.

Obviously, this is also a major advantage, decisions might take a little bit of time, but are most of the time correct and acceptable.

However; a person also doesn't know what type of feelings may bother after some cycle of time.

The most powerful advantage is these types of feelings can **sometimes rule over static feelings.**

So, what kind of feelings do you have? What do you think which is better? Are there any other crisp of feelings exists!

You are driven by my actions, And I won!

One can do two things in this case:

Win-Win Strategy:

Become *Friends*and stay forever!

Win-Lose Strategy:

Ignore that person, and you won!

But you hurt either one or bothof you.

But, it may help you to grow if that person is just a burden to you.

It's okay!

Not invited, it's okay.

Not considered, it's okay.

Emotionless for me, it's okay.

Not talking, it's okay.

Not having time, it's okay.

Your it's okay, it's okay.

Your problems is equal to my problems, it's okay.

As I want you to directly deep dive. So, it's okay.

Let me also share with you a random **Love Story :**

Will Make Him Forget Her!

Do you know you re quit intresting?

But why she doesn't pay attention to you?

It seems that she doesn't really care about you?

But why do you have to try to make her happy?

I saw you feel down because of her.

Do you know it's disturbing to see the way she treats you?

It's sad to see you get lonely.

What an adorable guy you are!

I think a person like you deserve a person like me.

I think we deserve each other.

You and I are a better match than you and her.

Let me love you and I will make you forget her.

It is such a waste of your opportunity.

You are such a good person but she doesn't appreciate you.

I have heared that we should love the one that love you.

Let me honest, loving me is so much a better choice.

I saw you feel down because of her.

It is sad to see you get lonely.

What an adorable guy you are!

You and I are better choice than you and her.

So, how do you deal with life situations, it is a set of either ups or downs. In the end, what actually matters, is **knowledge, its implementation, and happiness**.

So it is really okay if you cried today for some bad reason from your past. People come and go. Do you realize your role? How frequently till now you may be with somebody and the next moment of life, you are not! It is **LIFE**!

My messages for you!

Life is full of tremendous and fascinating things. Do you agree?

This chapter covers my personal thoughts from my experience till now, I am thankful and appreciate it if you go through it...

Now I listen old as well as new songs,

Still finding different meanings by

listening again and again!

Accepting a negative experience,

is a positive experience.

credits to whom so belong

No love might ever matter,

If I do not hug myself.

Without life my soul could never have this body.

I am very thankful to the nature for giving me this opportunity.

Let me be honest,

Love is the road that goes both ways.

I promise that I will always remember the school teachings.

Life is giving, so time has snatching capability.

A soul is different from body, so I do.

Everything doesn't happen coincidentally.

But coincidentally, everything can happen.

The Toxic Sip!

I took a sip from devils cup,

And now I am loosing.

The toxic sides of me are forcing,

to hide myself from the realities,

And enjoy the fantasies.

It's awesome, to see othersvcrying,

If I am the reason,
I may too cry, its my pleasure.

Do you want a sip from my cup?

Paradox of Thoughts

The more you **learn**, the more you realize how **little you know**!

"Life shrinks and expands in proportion to one's courage."
– Anais Nin

The more one learns to live, the less the fear of death!

Thinking, imaginations, dreams, and thoughts are the building blocks of one's life. So, the **more you think, the more you grow and the more you learn**!

But Is it true?

As we know, the more we use the equipment (or moving parts) there are higher the chances that it would become less useful more frequently.

But is it true in the case of mind too?

If we explore from a psychology point of view, the person is smart if he or she do not think too much and this actually results in a happier version of life.

As from "The Mindshift", our mind craves temptations, so is it really true not to think much!

If we explore ourselves from our childhood, even small things, actions and cartoons used to attract us, but when we become adults,

Why cartoons, festivals and those small actions do not make us feel pleasure and happiness like used to in our childhood?

The answer may vary, but my point is "Maturity".

So, are we really getting mature, if those things do not really affect us anymore?

I have observed many adults watching cartoons and kids watching adult and sex movies!

So, Is maturity really related to age?

The answer is perfect no! If you are not able to enjoy the moments of life as you were during your childhood, then your definition of maturity needs attention dear.

Thinking is actually important until it is productive and makes your every organ enjoy life!

If one is dynamic, loves to build a relationship with oneself from the past, then it is a good habit not to think much as it yields to OVERTHINKING!

And believe me, overthinking never yields good results.

For static personalities, they can easily deal with such situations and it is in their trait not to overthink until it is productive.

If someone says "I always lie," are they telling the truth? Or are they lying?

The great stoical logician Chrysippus came up with a paradox popularly known as the Liar Paradox.

It tells of a Cretan who sails to Greece. Upon arriving, he is greeted by Greek men on the shore and says, "All Cretans are liars." Did he speak the truth, or did he lie? A week later, the Cretan sails to Greece again and says, "All Cretans are liars and all I say is the truth."

The Greeks were truly puzzled. None were more confused than the grammarian and critic Philetus of Cos, who is said to have died of exhaustion while attempting to resolve the paradox.

Suppose your friend says, "He is coming to meet you tomorrow." Then, it is very simple to guess True or False! Like if he is absent his statement become false but if he comes to meet you, then the statement becomes true!

but what is the trueness if he comes to you, for a moment but leaves the place quickly? Yes! it is true to some extent but also seems to be false because it doesn't meet your expectations.

What do you think about the statement "**This ststement is false.**" statement is tue or false?

While solving the above, you may lie between true or false but not fully true or fully false!

So, do we feel this kind of paradox in our thoughts and then ignore them!

Like you have a feeling (a strong urge) to say hi to your crush, but what actually happens is the opposite!

Don't you feel the paradox in this case?

Actually, there exists no solution to this paradox but you may consider a third case other than being True or False as **NEITHER**.

What do you think about the following paradox of life:

1. Learn to love, not to hope.

2. Love is beautiful with hopes.

Lose! - A Love Story

Just an unexpected relationship for you,

but it's me who fell for it.

Just a flower grown to keep you entertained.

Just your makeshift lover to be left.

Can you explain it all, keep nothing hidden?

Can you answer me?

Waiting too long is frustrating. We can have enough and end it.

I know you just wanted me to fell into your trap of lies,

playing with my trust.

Even though you still have somebody else (still hiding).

Please answer my call, telling me you are still alive.

Please answer me, have no missed calls.

Please answer me, tell me you have someone else so that I might move on.

I am made for mistakes

A **soul**may be divided into two or four or as many parts as possible

only if it doesn't know itself!

Why does overthinking always yield negative thoughts?

Because our mind is negatively biased due to a lack of teachings about life.

The number one key to living life as we want is to explore life.

Do you know everybody has their own unique life story!

As we all know, overthinking nowadays becoming a critical issue.

What I have to say is actually it is not an issue that everybody elaborates it as full of negatives.

But, it depends on the status and training of the mind that we do in our life.

People do overthink good thoughts too. But, that is not harmful as it provides positive vibes in life.

Overthinking can actually yield better ideas in life if we understand for its reason.

So, if you are a static type of person, you know the value of overthinking. It is just like overclocking the CPU,in our case Brain.

1. Respect your space

What you want you should get

2. Communication is the key

Don't fall for games your mind can play

3. Take care of yourself

When nobody is there, you should be for yourself

I used to get **enthusiasm**and start praying for the **goodness**of others

until I got to know **many**are made for **destructio**n of others.

We call ourselves **human**and **dolphins**as animal.

Where, we believe:

Human= Respect and full of all goodness possible

Animal = Cruel, ugly and harmful

* (Human = Animal) is contradicting.

Learning is never ending process, but life is!

Change Society Change!

We need to understand that there is the importance of everything nature created.

Stop comparing success with masculine things only. There are psychologically different needs of both genders which ultimately creates a difference in the definition of success in both genders.

Neglecting one of the genders means neglecting society development and which ultimately affects the whole nation.

Once Somebody asked to "Joseph Campbell - Mythologist" :

What do you say about girls journey in life?

Girls are already in position,

Where males are trying to reach.

The girl who understand this,

will never try to become a **pseudo male**.

To be a female is not a weakness,

She teaches males how to love,

Courage the society to grow,

and motivates in tough times.

What do you think about the importance of **males psychologically**?

From traditional beliefs:

1. Males are considered to be a sole income source for the family.

2. To display traditional masculine traits like "strength" and "control".

3. To be fully dependent on oneself and do not seek help from others.

4. **To not to speak openly about their emotions.**

These are the unique and different factors from females that directly affect the mental health of males.

Yes! Man do have stressful life events. They may also have passed through traumatic life events.

I love my life!

Yes, you have lots of happiness,

Yes, you have lots of sadness,

Lots of hope with full of disagreements,

Lots of struggle with lots of failure,

But I am okay to survive.

I would never not stop trying,

Because I love you my life.

Anything that is truly mine.

is you my life.

I love my life.

Feelings and Physics

Don't worry, physics complex formulas are ignored here! But a big thank you to all physics contributors.

As we have already discussed the static and dynamic concepts of feelings in "Strategy of thoughts".

Observe yourself sitting calm, independent your mind to only think about you.

No external relationships.

No worries of job or studies.

Just for a moment, consider no food!

Just you and you and you!

Nobody else!

What do you feel? Alone, calm, you rule the world, the universe is craving to protect you and since there is nobody, you are only left for yourself!

So, now in what category of feeling do you fall? Static or Dynamic!

Just think for a minute before reading further.

In both or none might be your answer. And this is the stage where nobody has the perfect answer.

Just observe the below text carefully:

Like, when you are writing a big story, but at other time you wanted to erase one of the whole page,

But their are still some elements like dots and some ignored smaller marks left.

Just like same, Can we consider the universe too?

Those left peices are lives that might exist in universe!

So, to what extent it is true. It might practically seem to be true from the fact that the universe is expanding and chances that there might exist other lives too! So, can you explain why the energy that is erasing something might be life? What must go wrong?

Psychologically, the above statement seems to lie between true and false. To some extent, it seems true and to others is false!

Have a deep thinkng, take your time to lead yourself to one of the conclusion.

It seems to be difficult, but it actually depends on your views of life. So, answers are different for everyone.

It seems to be a kind of paradox situation you might go through. But doesn't it makes **life itself a paradox**!

We have a limited time of life expectancy, with millions of unbreakable puzzles.

That might be only solved if we transfer knowledge from one generation to other.

Yes! there might exist a dangerous rule of time.

What do you think of feelings being physically dependent or independent?

The field of physics is too vast to explore to get these answers perfectly.

People with good emotional health are aware of their thoughts, feelings and behaviour.

Taking care of yourself, having positive thoughts, improves the immune system.

Our body cells behave the way we think. Like when we are happy, we feel positive emotions and our body health improves considerably but when we are sad, we feel physical chest pains too.

One should consider the following:

1. The ways to cope from stress. Believe me, when you tackle the actual reason and sharing your emotions with others helps a lot.

2. Just observe yourself, if stress might be due to the physical health or some past trauma.

3. If everything in the life running smoothly, **why still you are not happpy**?

Be forgiving to yourself, do not give pain and stress to yourself. It is a record that nothing good has happened by following pains in life. People become successful by working on their pains.

If there are 114 million people, then there are 114 million unique ways to the divine energy.

At the end of life,

everything seems to be fake.

But what actually matters,

are the intentions throughout living.

If we are projects

So, they will take birth and die with time?

How would you still manage then?

They will eat other accordingly as rules.

Oh! Great plan. It acttually fits in everything, but there is a big bug,

what about new born and physically weak species.

Thats's why I added feelings there.

There is no such great issues. However, strongness is preferred.

Still,if weak one would manage feelings, they could survive too.

Good game sir!

But if there are bugs.

Meteors would handle that.

No worries.

It's time to submit this project.

The Brain

This chapter is dedicated and inspired from "Introduction to Psychology - By Yale University".

This chapter will dive you into certain psychological philosophies and theories. These would help you to understand the importance of mind, thinking process and effect of thoughts in real life.

This is a story about a man named Phineas Gage. He was a blasting foreman working on a railway construction project, his job was to clear the way of rocks to lay down the tracks. He used to blast the rocks by digging a hole in them then put some powder stuff along with some sand and using a piece of steel, which seems to be a javelin so that later they could set the fuse and cause the explosions.

But one day, when he was putting javelin the rock exploded. The tamping iron shot away from his hand and went into his face. It entered the left side of Gage's jaw, moving in an upward direction, it passed behind the left eye through the left side of the brain, it went out to the top of his skull and landed several feet away from the clutter.

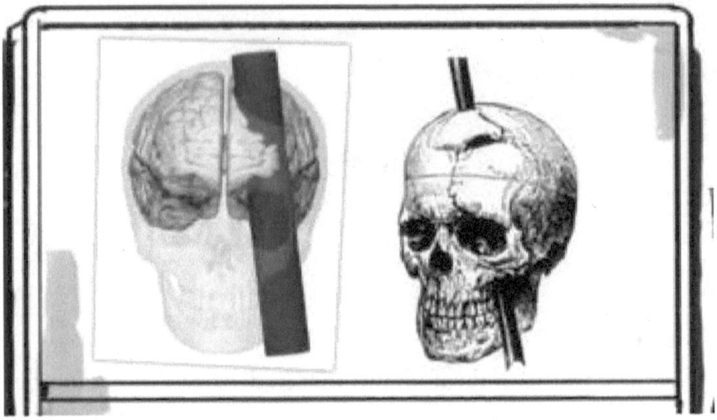

credits: Yale University

But he wasn't dead on the spot. He lost his consciousness a little bit, but then he staggered to his feet.

He was got hurt physically, got lots of treatment, he got sick but with time he was recovered. He was recovered to normal vision, he was able to hear and he wasn't paralyzed, was able to speak and understand.

But there were tremendous changes in his nature:

Before incident -

He was the most efficient and capabale man with temperate habits. Considerable energy of character and a sharp shrewd businessman.

After incident -

He was fitful, irrevelant, indulging at times in the grossest profanity, manifesting but little deference for his fellows.

The brain is a source of mental life. So, the damaged brain can have profound effects on who we are and what we are.

The idea here is given by the noble prize-winning biologist Francis Crick, he calls it "**The Astonishing Hypothesis**".

The Astonishing Hypothesis

The Astonishing Hypothesis is that "You," your joys and your sorrows, your memories and your ambitions, your sense of personal identity and free will, are in fact no more than the behaviour of a vast assembly of nerve cells and their associated molecules.

As we know we all are materialistic. The official term for this is materialism that we are material beings. Our arms, legs, heart and kidneys are made of the same sort of stuff as rabbits and automobiles and cups. But what makes us different is our mental life, most intimate feelings and thoughts.

So, we are what our mind makes us? what are our thoughts in a certain life situation?

People may have similar life goals, but what makes difference is views, life situations and ultimately the thoughts and feelings for the goal.

What do you think about the scope of statement "**brain = mind**"?

It is **radical**.

As we know, t**he brain is a part of our body**. But what **dualism**in psychology beliefs is **the body and the mind exist as separate entities**.

So, if materialism is right, not only don't we have souls but maybe there is no such thing as souls, or to put it in a different way, there is no such thing as mental life separate from the body.

For example, if somebody dies, their simply brain stopped working and he or she is gone out of life.

The brain seems to be like a computer of 0s and 1s. The mind is an information processor. And we treat the brain as the physical aspect of the hardware and our mental lives, the ideas, our processes, our heuristics, our algorithms as the software, as the programs that this hardware runs.

This way looking at things, it works extremely well when it comes to activities like face recognition, language, motor control, logic and so on.

But there still remains what philosopher David Chalmers has called t**he hard problem of consciousness**.

The feeling of what it is to slam your hand in a car door, eat scrambled eggs with a lot of sauce, have an orgasm, grieve for the death of your friend etc., The feeling of what it's like, the qualia that many people believe can not be simulated on a computer.

This is the power of the uncertainity. You can explore more in the course.

Ideal cases

If considering facts, no full ideal cases are possible.

There are uncertain elements left even when a maximum of the target activity is achieved.

Practically, no full ideal cases are possible.

So,

Do love, hate, apathy, dedicated relationships exist!

Because all of them seems to be ideal cases.

Do complete living exist!

Life is also an ideal case in-universe, so found only on one planet.

But it exists, at least on one planet.

So, does all of them exist in a very little amount?

Are we still struggling to find them?

Or, we have found and hiding in ourselves!

A nerd love story again...

Tired

Monday, I am waiting.

Tuesday, I'm still waiting to see.. see..

If you are fine..

Wednesday, you are still here.

Neither in the morning, nor later.

Thursday is also empty.

Friday, Saturday or even Sunday,

None of the day that I don't missed you.

None of the day, that you will come back.

To be in our old days.

The days, I was close to you.

The day, when we did handshake.

The days, I loved you.

The days, we understood each other.

Might now never come.

Note: These stories are for entertainment purpose only.

Psychology facts

This is the collection of psychology facts that might be very helpful to you:

There will always be a reason why you meet people. Either you need them to change your life or you are the one who helps to change theirs.

It takes up-to five positive things to outweigh one negative thing.

Attention Deficit Hyperactivity Disorder (ADHD) often begins in childhood and can persist into adulthood.

It may contribute to low self-esteem, troubled relationships and difficulty at school or work.

Worst thing about this is you need to identify it by yourself.

The average person has 3 to 5 best friends, and usually hates one person in their social group.

A psychological study has found that people who are generally "TOO NICE" are also the ones who gets "EMOTIONAL HURT THE MOST".

If we have plan B, our plan A is less likely to work. With options, our motivation to succeed the first time drops.

Every day, the heart creates enough energy to drive a truck 20 miles. In a lifetime, that is equivalent to driving to the moon and back.
So, when you tell someone you love them "to the moon and back" you're essentially saying you will love them with all the blood your heart pumps your whole life, which I think is equally as meaningful.

Friendship means UNDERSTANDING, not agreement.
It means FORGIVENESS, not forgetting.
It means the MEMORIES last, even if contact is lost.

Remember that people will always question the good things they hear about you, and believe the bad ones without a second thought.

Dogs can see sadness in humans and often attempt to make their owners happy by initiating cuddling.

You can find daily facts on the Instagram page (openlyclose).

Thank you!

I am very thankful to you if you read the book fully and tried to understand each chapter.
I really hope you also enjoyed the unique content of my book.

All this content is self-created with some motivation to share my thoughts with you. So, I really hope you understand the copyright rules, and sharing, editing, recopying, republishing the book is totally prohibited without written permission from the owner.

Thank you!
Have a great day!

www.ingramcontent.com/pod-product-compliance
Lightning Source LLC
LaVergne TN
LVHW100338181026
850499LV00039B/1125
* 9 7 8 9 3 5 6 1 0 1 7 4 6 *